ISBN 978-0-9933626-1-3

Publisher: Westbury Arts Centre, UK
Poetry editor: Helen denDulk
Design: Ivana Kucirkova
Creative direction: Kate Wyatt and Eleni Cay
Printed by: IngramSpark
First printed: September 2015

Introduction

Ekphrastic poetry (from the Greek word ekphrasis meaning "for the sake of pointing out") is poetry that verbally describes a visual work of art.

Poetry and watercolour painting connect on many levels, but for Kate's and my work is mostly in terms of the rhythm and colours we use for composing.

Kate starts with big pencil marks, then steps back, lets them rest for a while, then later edits them down.

We both agonise over one specific shade, one exact word, then add one more line, one more dot, delete it, come back and sometimes, reluctantly, release the piece to the wild.

We tend to use a limited palette to convey our feelings; somehow, a few words or a few colours, give us more control to find what we are looking for and more freedom to escape the everyday.

For both of us, swans symbolise the power of colour cycles which, from pure white Odette to deep black Odile, sustain life and grant presence to other colours.

Swans have always played an important part in my life, spellbinding me into reverie with their layered tutus, floating on water like lilies.

Kate gave them new colours, granted them spider web- bodies filled with mosaic decoration.

This collection is our humble expression of the admiration we hold for swans and the truth, loyalty and elegance they stand for.

Eleni Cay, February, 2015

About this collection

In Colours of the Swan, the two artists come together juxtaposing their mediums, creating a piece of art which celebrates the connections between magic and life, colours and words, freedom to imagine and obligation for authentic representation.

Using a unique mix of hues and shapes, words and metaphors, Eleni and Kate imagine their swans into meanings which augment each other, reaching levels of meaning they could not convey with their individual mediums.

Eleni's poems respond to Kate's eight paintings, bound by the theme of swans gradually changing colours.

The continuum of a white-black transformation of the swans sequence is framed by two dominant birds (The Crane Wife and Isis).

All names of the paintings and titles of the poems are inspired by ancient civilisations or Gaelic words.

Artist's short biographies

Eleni Cay

Eleni's first collection, ''A butterfly's shivering in the digital age' which is written in Slovakian,
was published after she won a national poetry competition in her native country Slovakia.
Eleni's selected English language poems appeared in several anthologies and magazines and have been
also recreated as filmpoems. The ekphrastic poetry with Kate Wyatt reflects the breadth of Eleni's work,
characterised by careful adherence to traditional poetic forms and innovative use of new media, giving rise
to truly authentic pieces.

Kate Wyatt

Kate is an artist and illustrator, one of the UK's leading wildlife painters with work in many galleries
throughout the world and in private collections. Unlike her wildlife paintings, Kate's Shamanic works do
not aim to reproduce reality but rather, reflect the mystical world of shamans, with their magical powers.
To paint this series, Kate used a carefully selected palette of colours: Gold, Indigo, Cadmium yellow, Cobalt
blue, Alizarin purple, Emerald Green, Crimson and Yellow Ochre. She always knew that London, with its
creative pedigree and broad vision, would be the ideal place for these powerful statement pieces.

Contents page

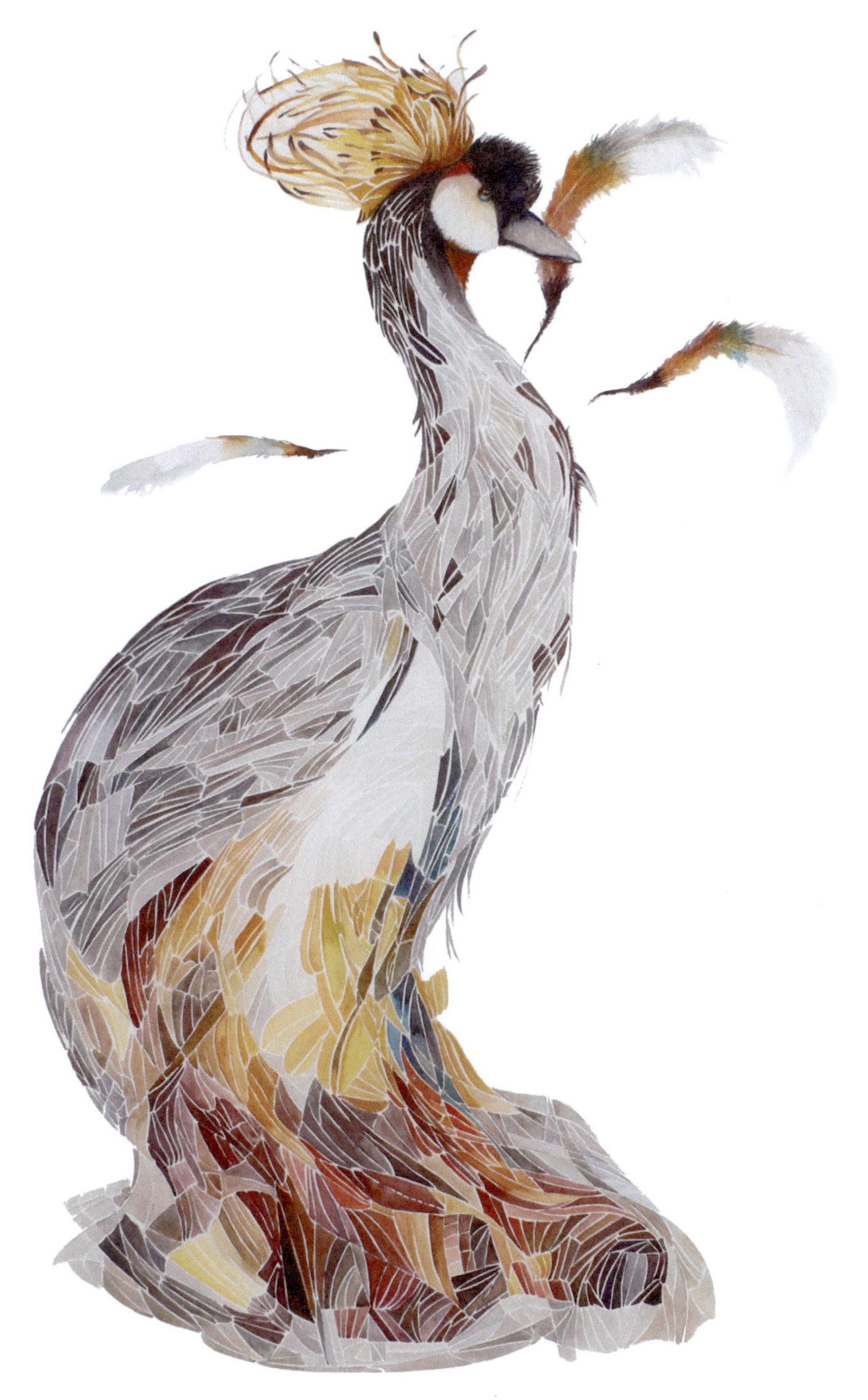

Crane Wife

Setting your breast forward,
you walk on the grass like royals
who do not mix with the commoners.

You would do anything to be unlike others -

You steal beauty from coveted hives.
You cut your arteries to bleed in darker colours.

You would even fake to be ratite,
pluck out your most precious feathers.

So that your admirers can pick them up.
And let your soul glide to heavens.

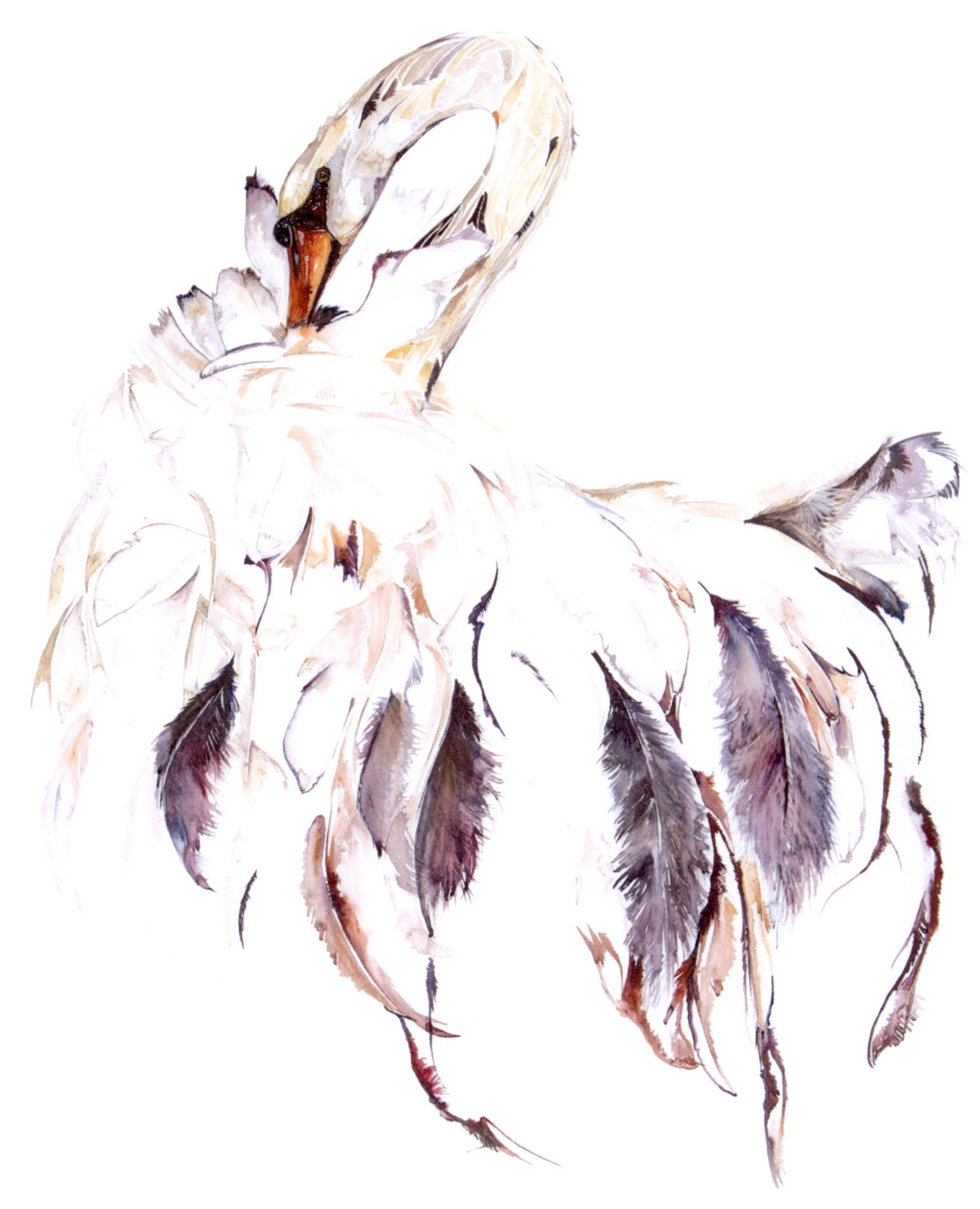

Odile/ Odette

The Prince thought her whiteness would shine
like water lilies in the deep night.
Or snowdrops in the dark forest.

But when her petals fell away,
he did not know the precise shade of white
dividing Lotus from Odette.

The Queen of the Swans vanished in grey,
leaving behind a strange silhouette.

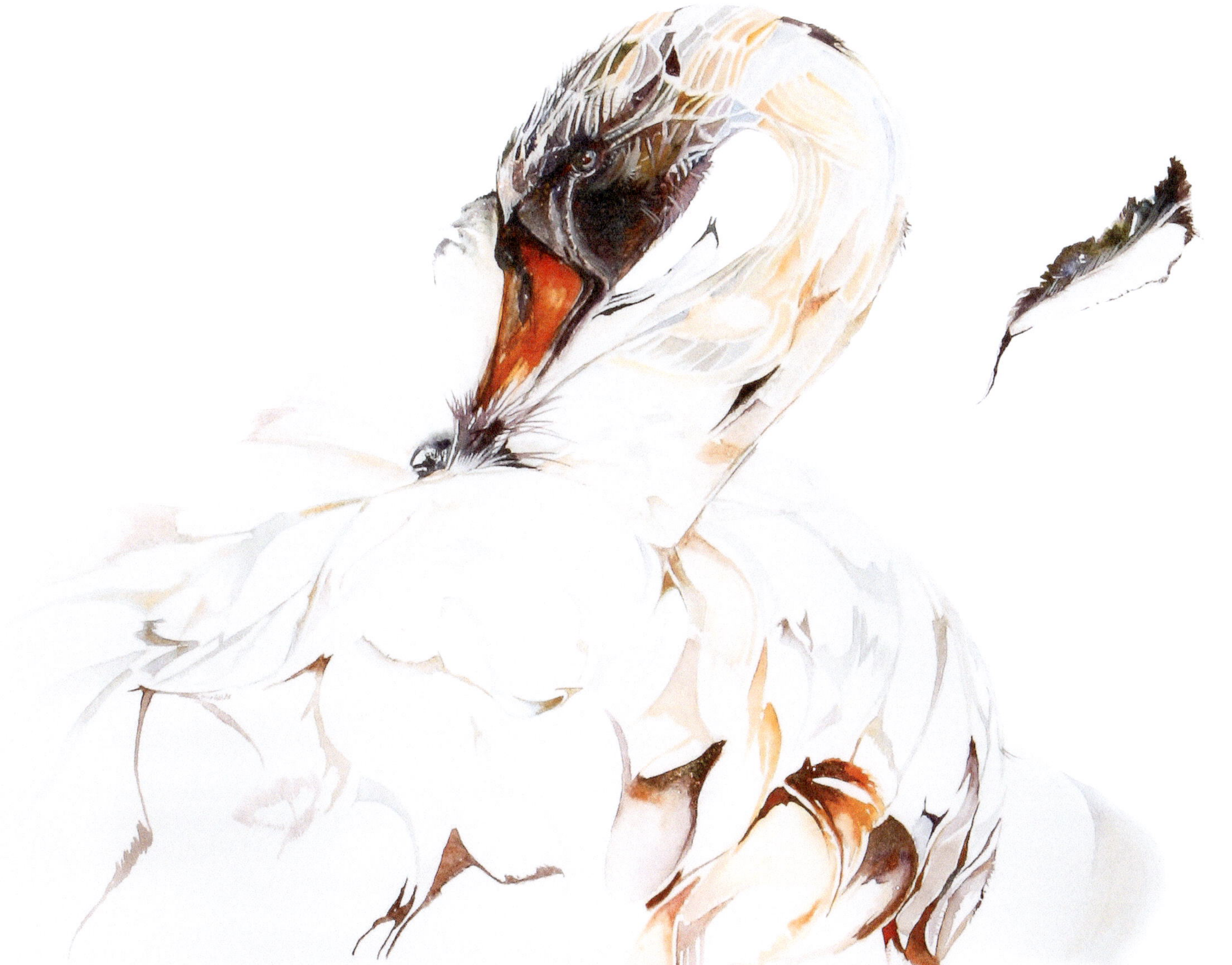

Iseult

Hybrid creature
has lost her home twice.

She doesn't belong to the waters,
she doesn't belong to the skies.
Since Adam and Eve sinned,
she has been the child of the shore.

Wishing that she could give a voice to trees,
She molted her fluffed feathers, selflessly,
all the way to the skin's core.

Yearning for an ever-lasting romance
she rests in expectation, enveloped in her colourful dreams.

But all she ever receives is a puff, an ephemeral fragrance
of the fig leaves.

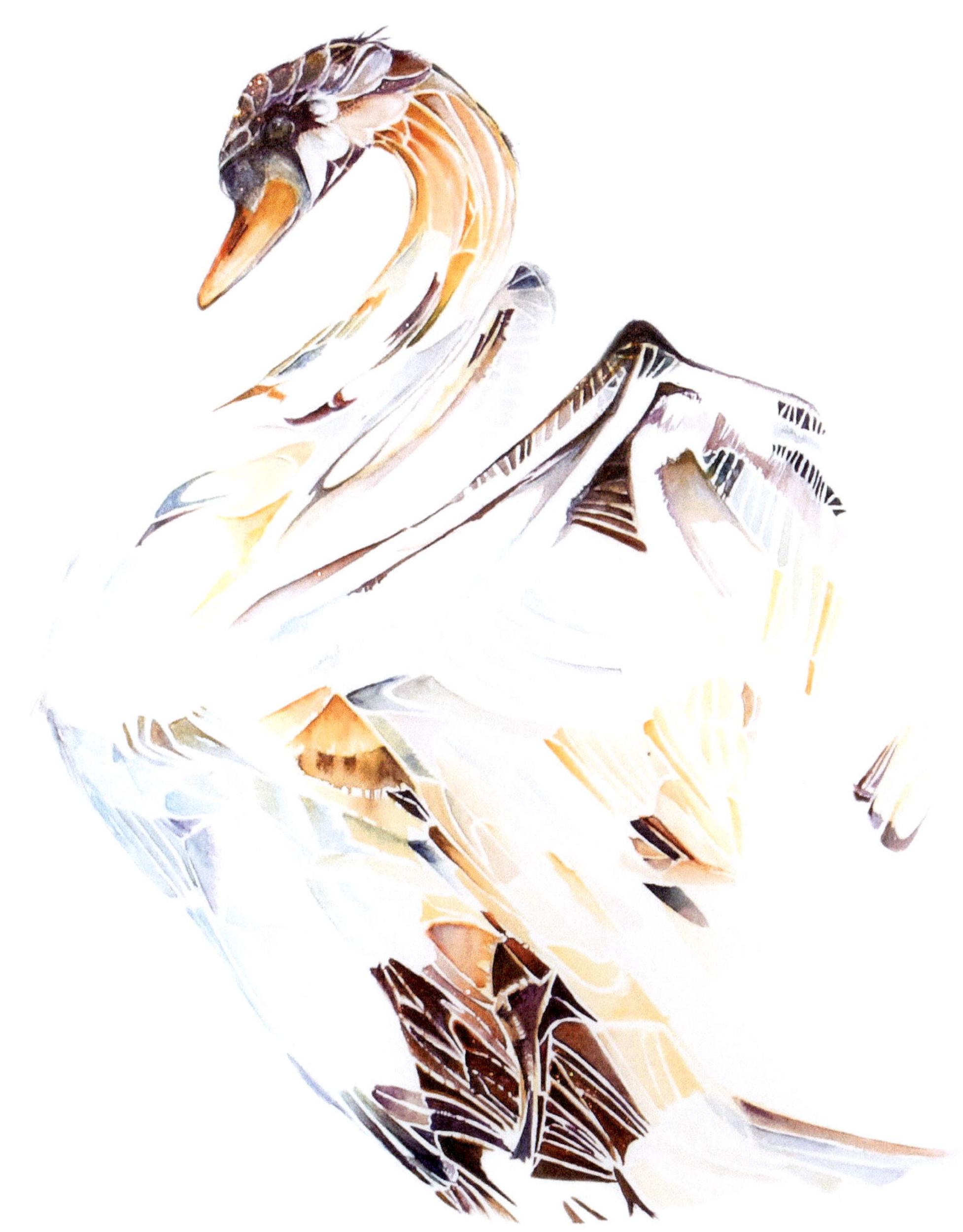

Teagan [1]

You never knew about my secret life.
Why I would at times disappear, lock myself up
in a dark, cold room, obliterate my own feathers.

You never understood how I would lose myself
to shamanic guidance, and yet control carefully
every single hue I had shed.

You thought I had been unfaithful to you.
Or that I had an illness.

One day, you broke into my cage,
wrenched apart all the chains.

But all you could find were unfinished threads,
beginning in me and finishing in others.

You looked at me in astonishment -

You never knew I was a poet.

---

1 Teagan is the diminutive of the Irish "tadhg" which means poet.

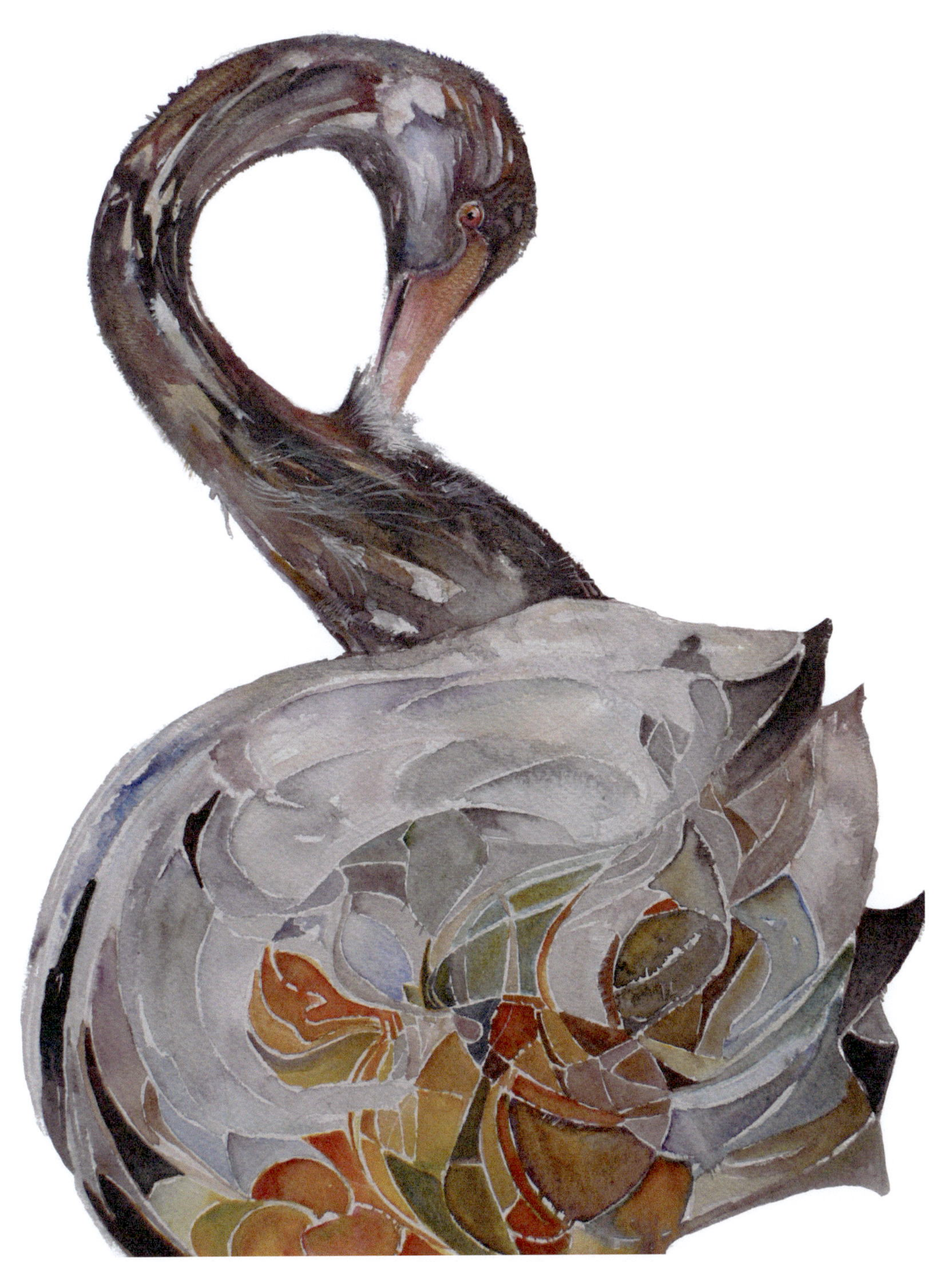

Niamh [1]

Your wild dreams crawl, from the wind-broken stalk
to your small black pupil, shining like a jewel
against a black cloth.

With those spangles you strike a narrow opening
in timelessness. And give everyday encounters
more worth.

Others try to emulate your style
but only you can glide so elegantly
on the mundane.

When you let flow your golden song,
I'm in awe. All the way from the little toe to the tongue.

---

1   In Irish mythology, Niamh is the daughter of the God of the sea and one of the queens of the land of eternal youth, the name also means radiant or bright.

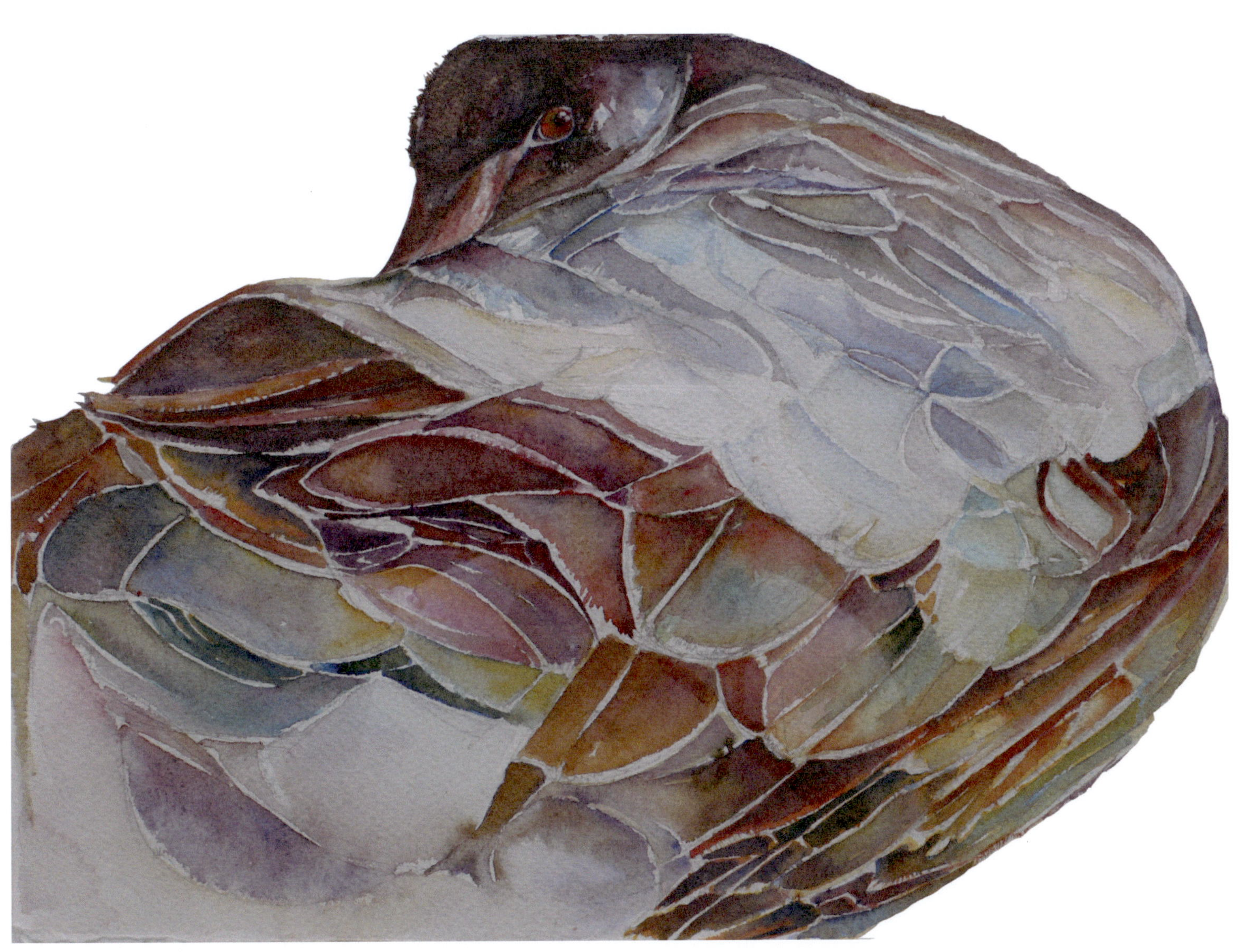

Roisin[1]

They told you that all fairy tales
have a beginning, middle and an end.

They didn't tell you that in love,
there are no boundaries.

That sky is made of small twisted lines
of transparent paint.

That behind the sunset,
passion never disappears.

That one image is more than thousand words
and louder than the cry of the sirens.

That the most beautiful moment
is when we let dragonflies land on us
- in silence.

---

1 Roisin means little rose and is a common Irish female name.

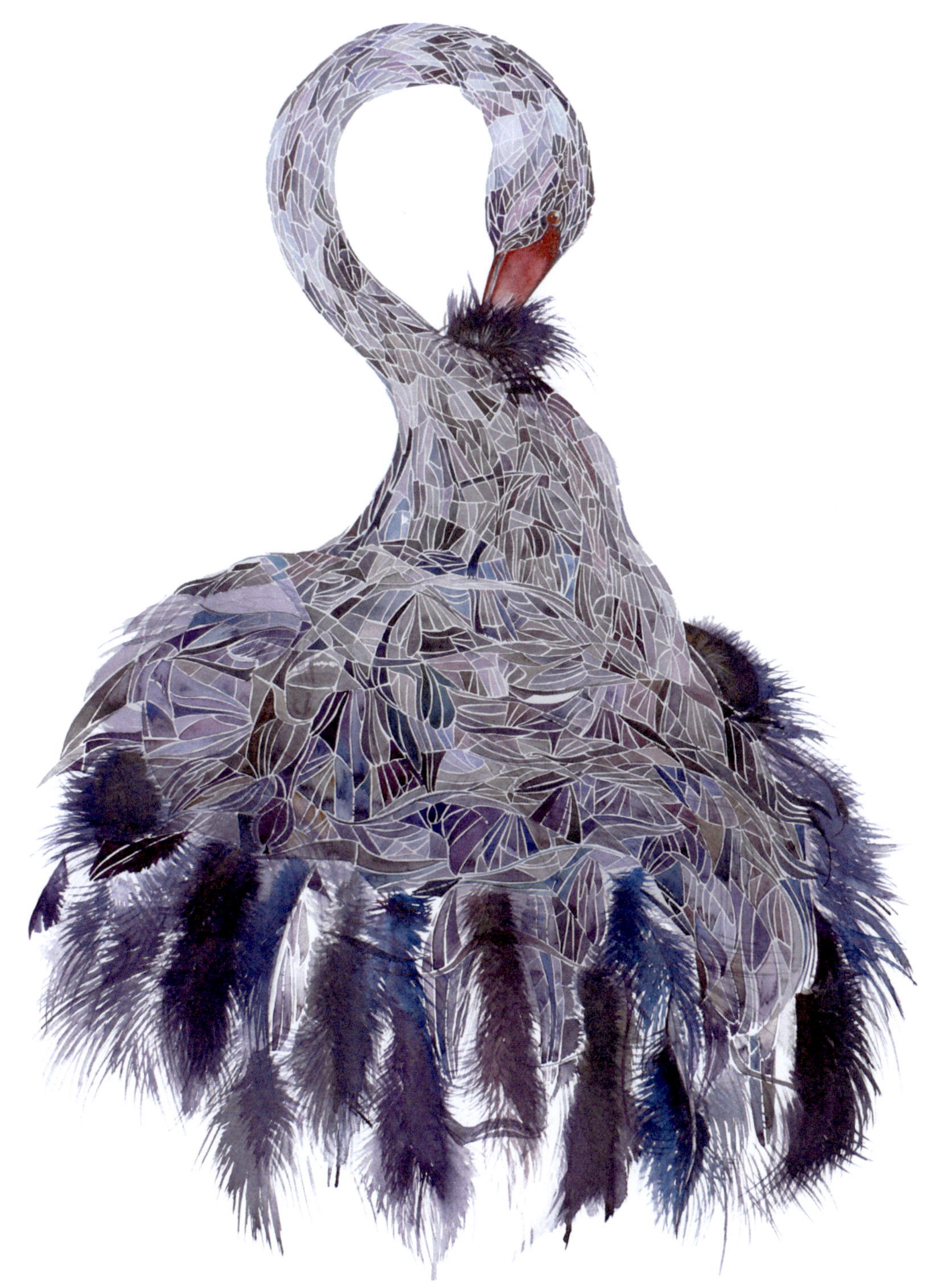

Black Swan

In deep caverns of human souls, where only embers
from the dark coal shine, the Devil forges
raven-winged thoughts.

In sizzling smoke, he preens virgin feathers,
puts them into the mouths of newborns till they choke,
nails them to the bottom of their hearts, grinning.

He assails them, till they start wheezing like hyenas,
bleeding their evil into the never-ending opening
between the Earth and the skies.

He baits millions and millions of broken shards
with glistering white, lets them tear through human lives,
promise love, but then, like a fickle chameleon
deeply bites, chucking them out,
to grieve alone.

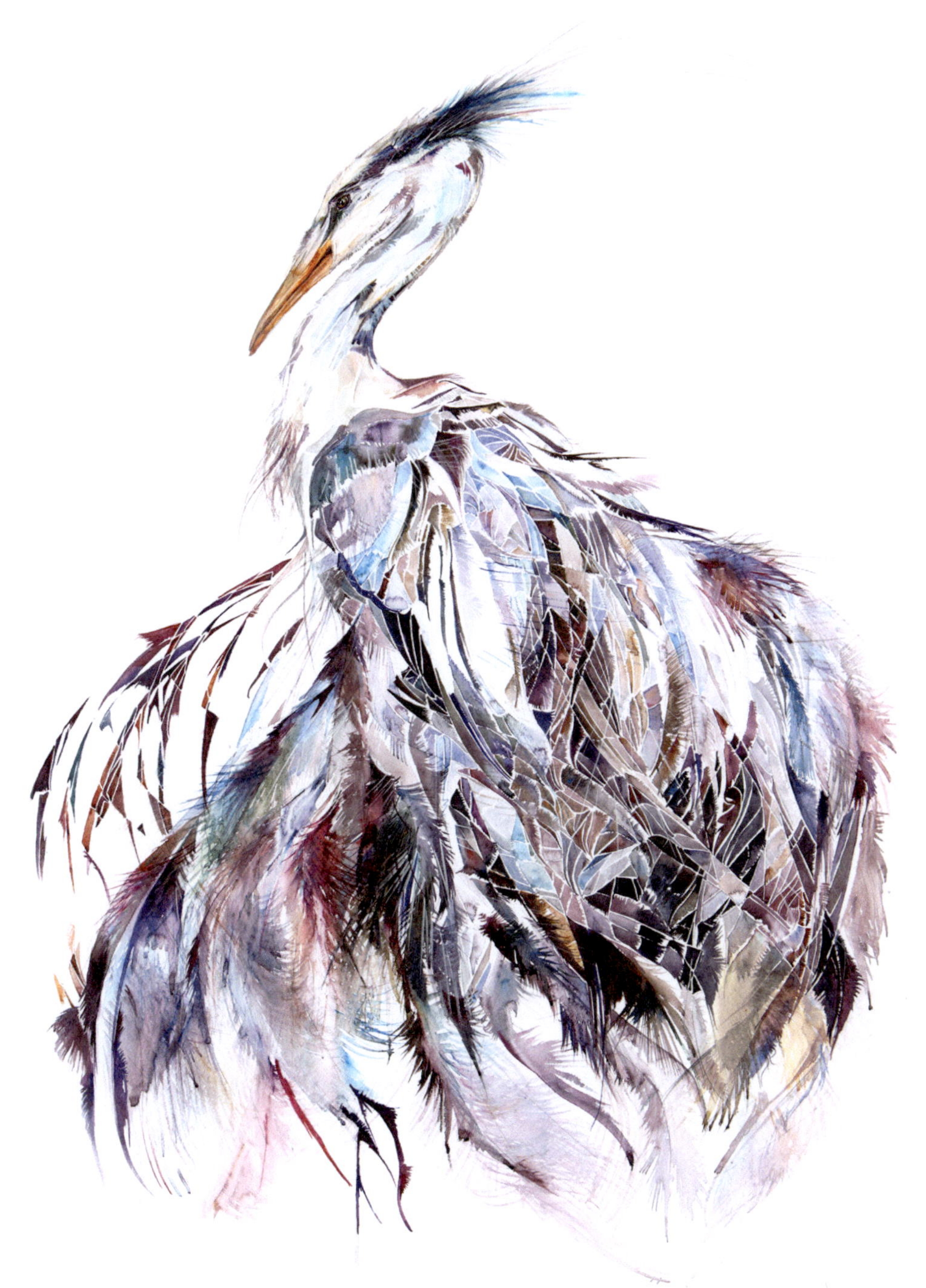

Isis

She bestows blush pink sweetness and golden hues upon your ruffled life,
until you re-imagine yourself into mounds of branching possibilities,
covered in clouds of tiny flowers scenting like a baby's skin.

She turns the pain of an opera singer
into a lullaby, fondly rocks you in dusky green afternoons.

She smoothens your rough edges,
takes out all the sharpness from your wounds,
relentlessly flooding your shores with kindness.

You want to drink sweetness from her breasts,
delicious like pistachio macarons.

You want to worship her, like a saint, floating above you,
loving and yet powerful like the Sun.

You know she is the one. You get on your knees,
you beg to lead to the altar
the Goddess Isis.

Printed by Libri Plureos GmbH in Hamburg,
Germany